Delicious Desserts
Coloring Book

An Adult Coloring Book Featuring Fun, Sweet and Delicious Desserts for Stress Relief and Relaxation

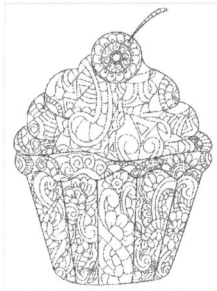

PUBLISHED BY THE FRUITFUL MIND LTD.

COLORING BOOK
Cafe

Disclaimer

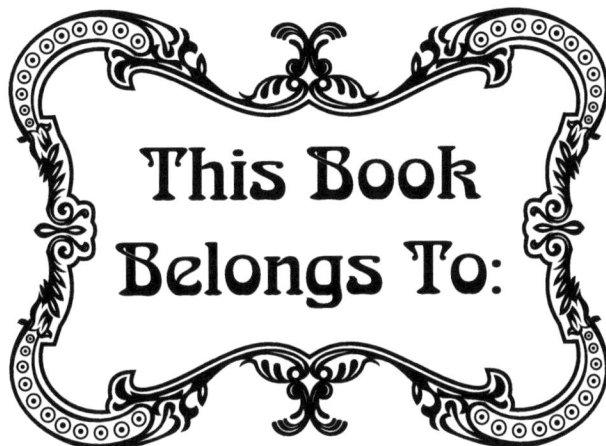

This Book
Belongs To:

BONUS

Relax And Create Your Own Masterpiece With
***THIS 10 PAGE FREE** Beautiful Adult Coloring Book*

Claim Your FREE Coloring Book at:

www.freecoloringbooklet.com

<u>**Samples Below**</u>

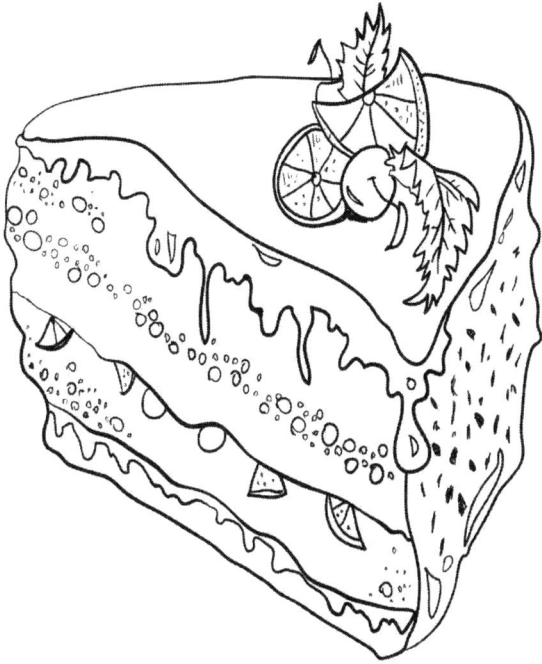

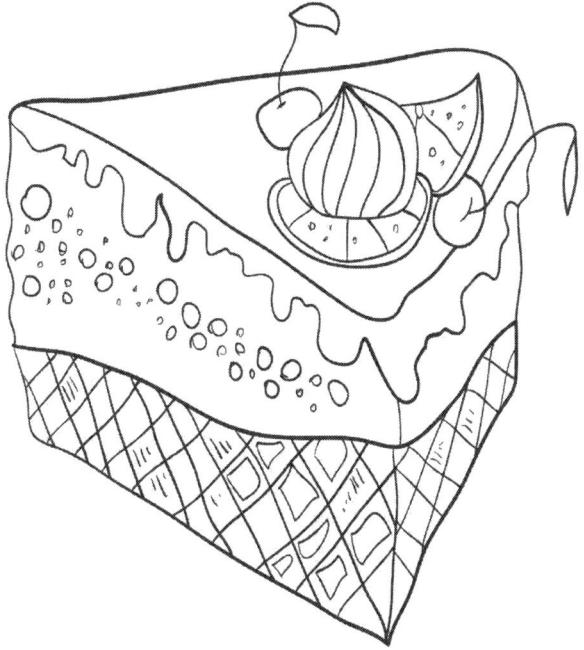

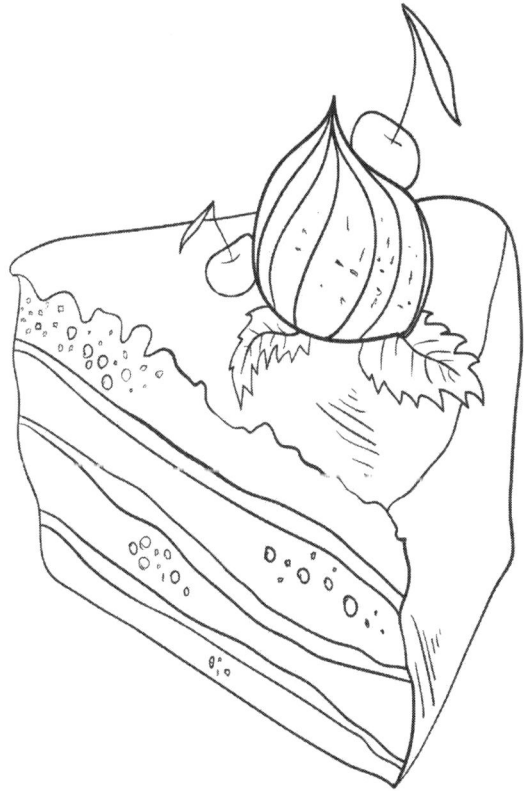

.

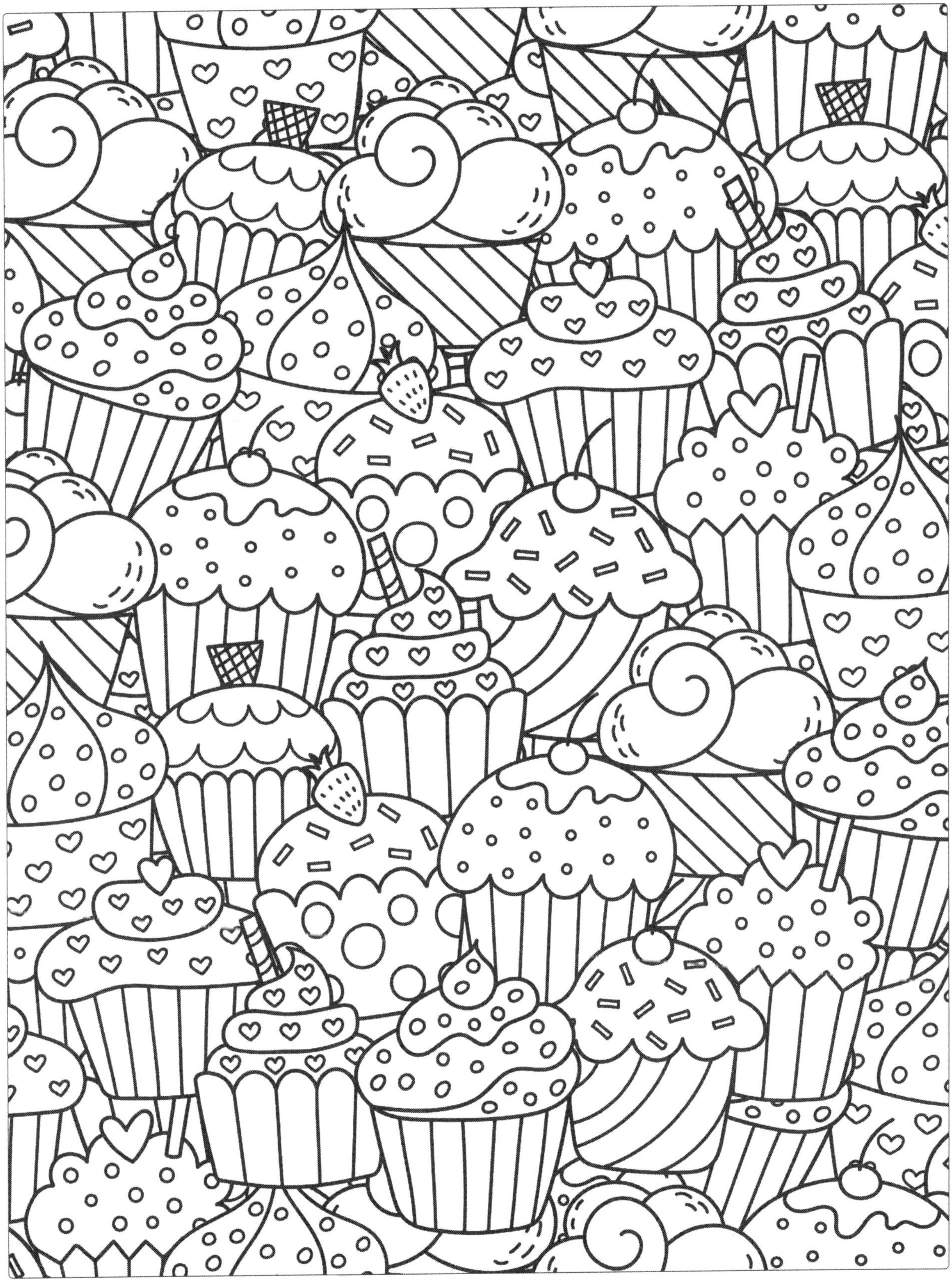

Manufactured by Amazon.ca
Bolton, ON

24279797R00037